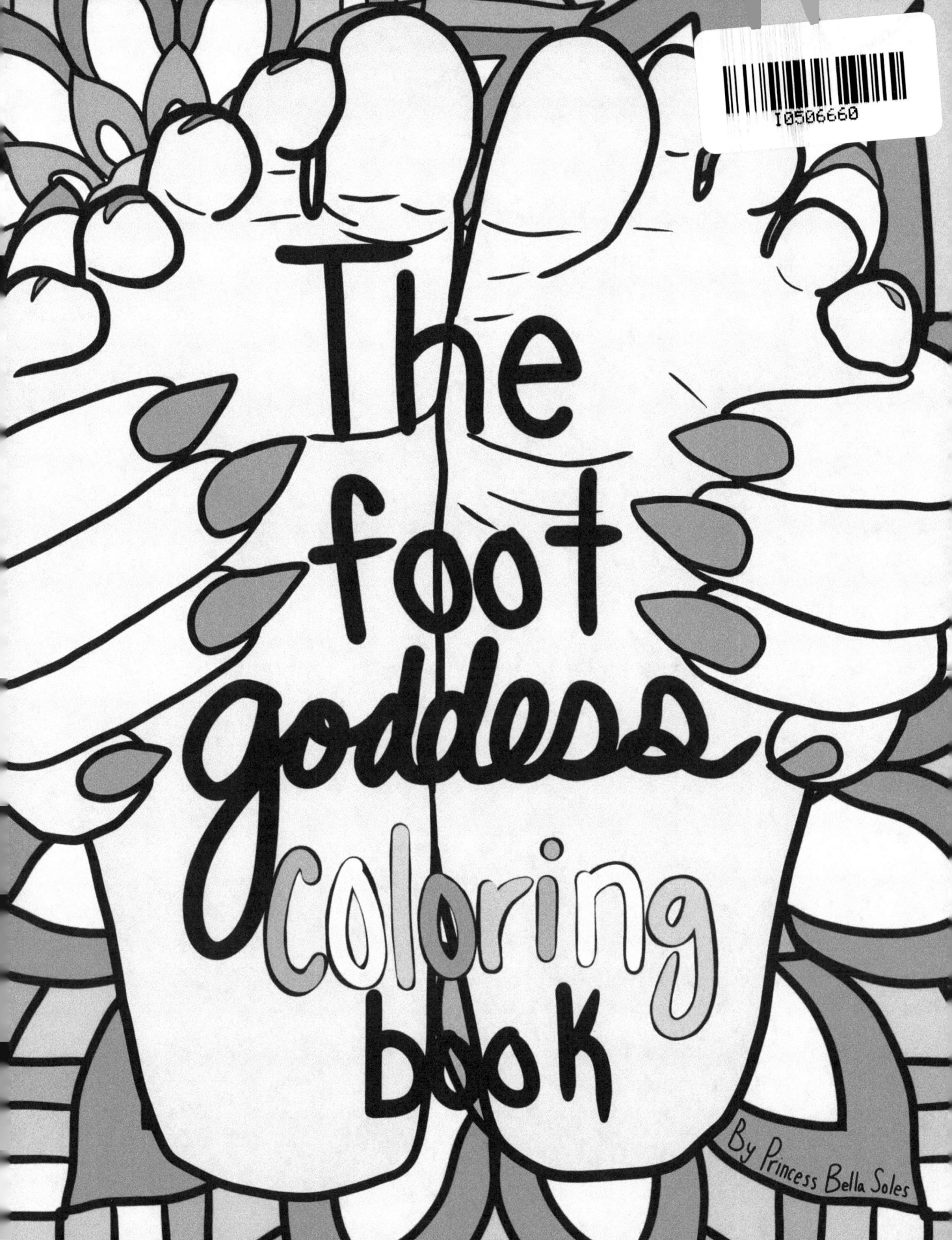

The Foot Goddess Coloring Book
Princess Bella Soles

All photographs used as reference for this book were taken by Princess Bella Soles. Each page in this book was hand drawn from those reference photos.

This is an adult book. The contents of this book are not to be offered for sale or reproduced in any way. You may not alter the book or the book's contents and sell it. Please enjoy this book for yourself and do not copy, transfer, share, or redistribute this book in any way.

© Princess Bella Soles

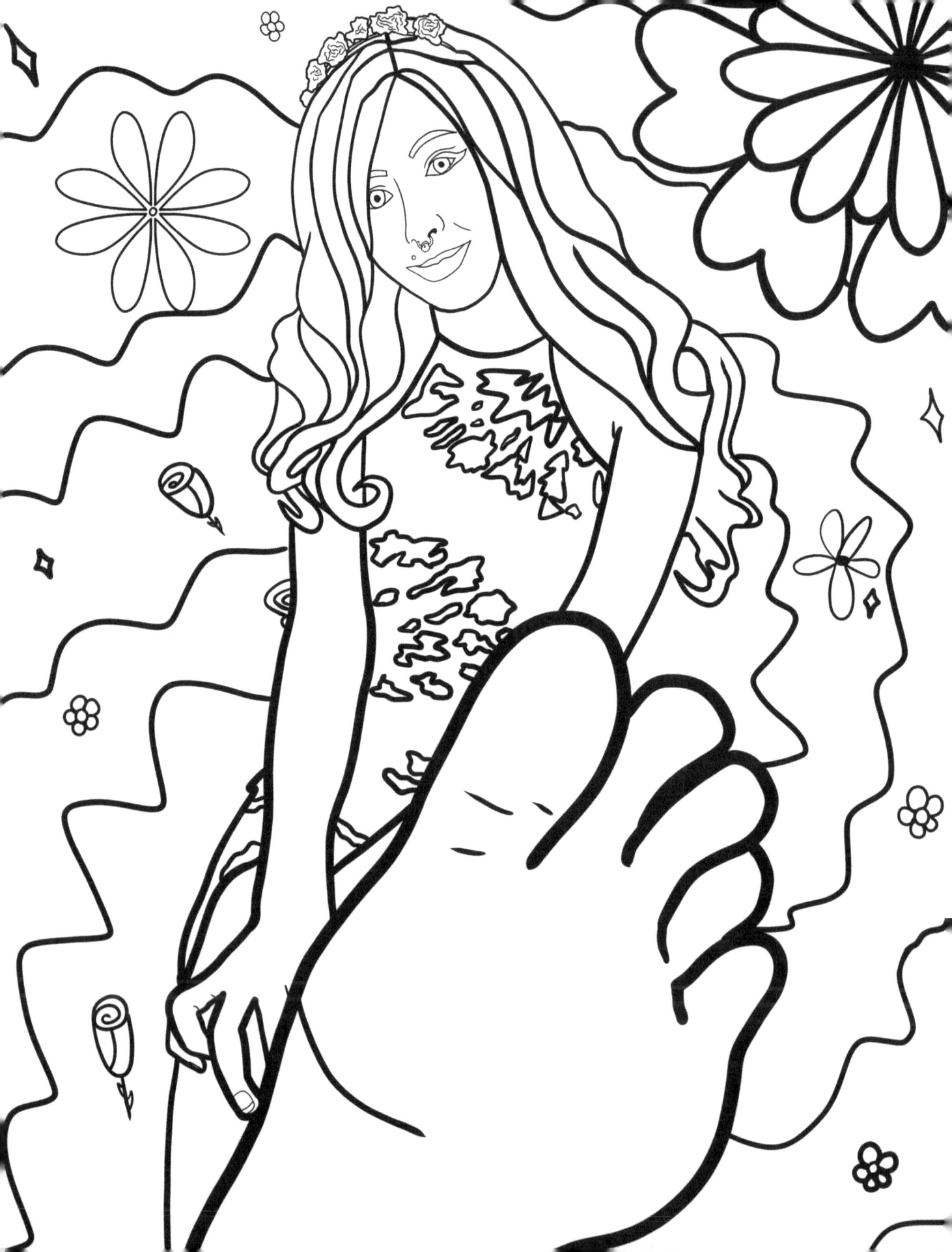

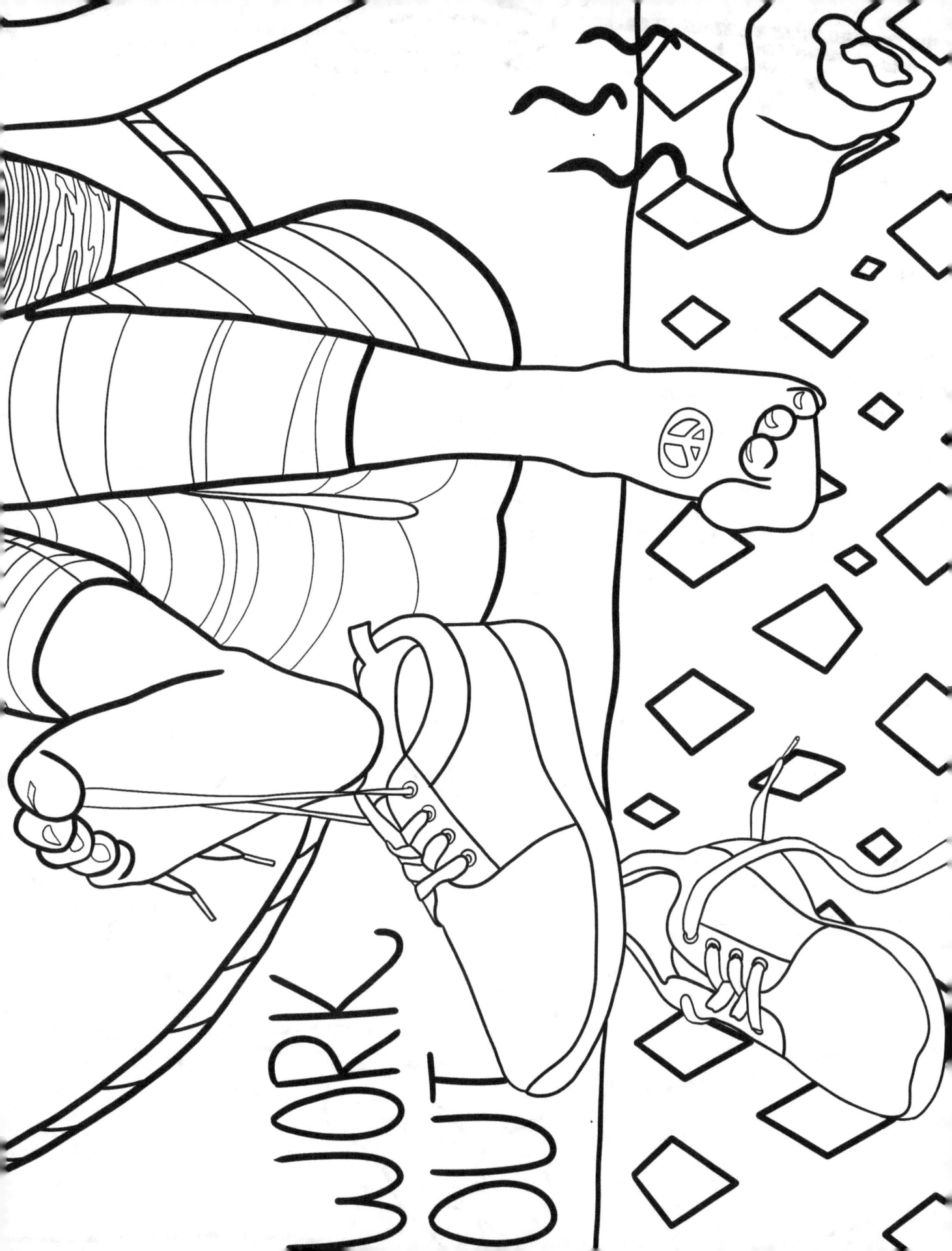

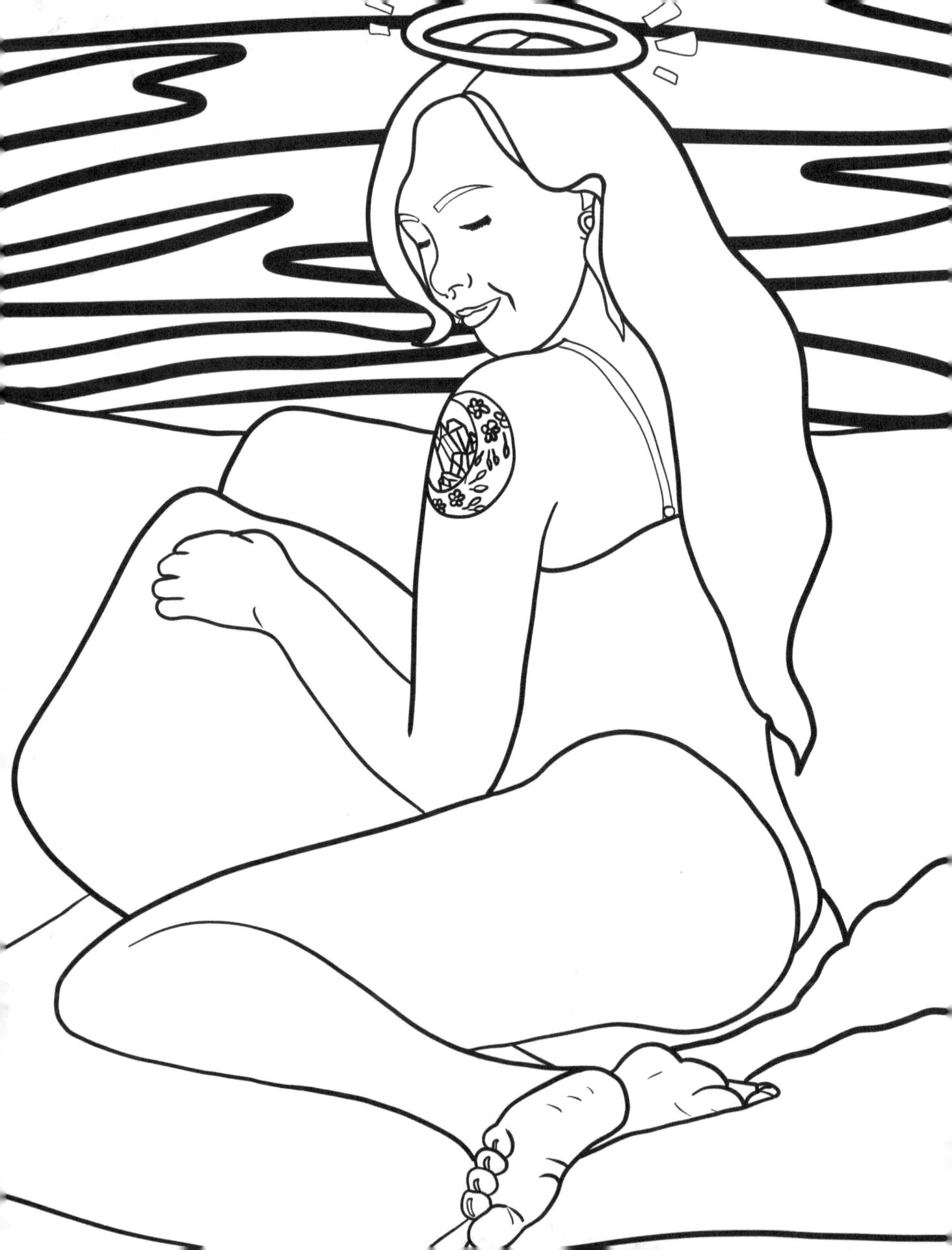

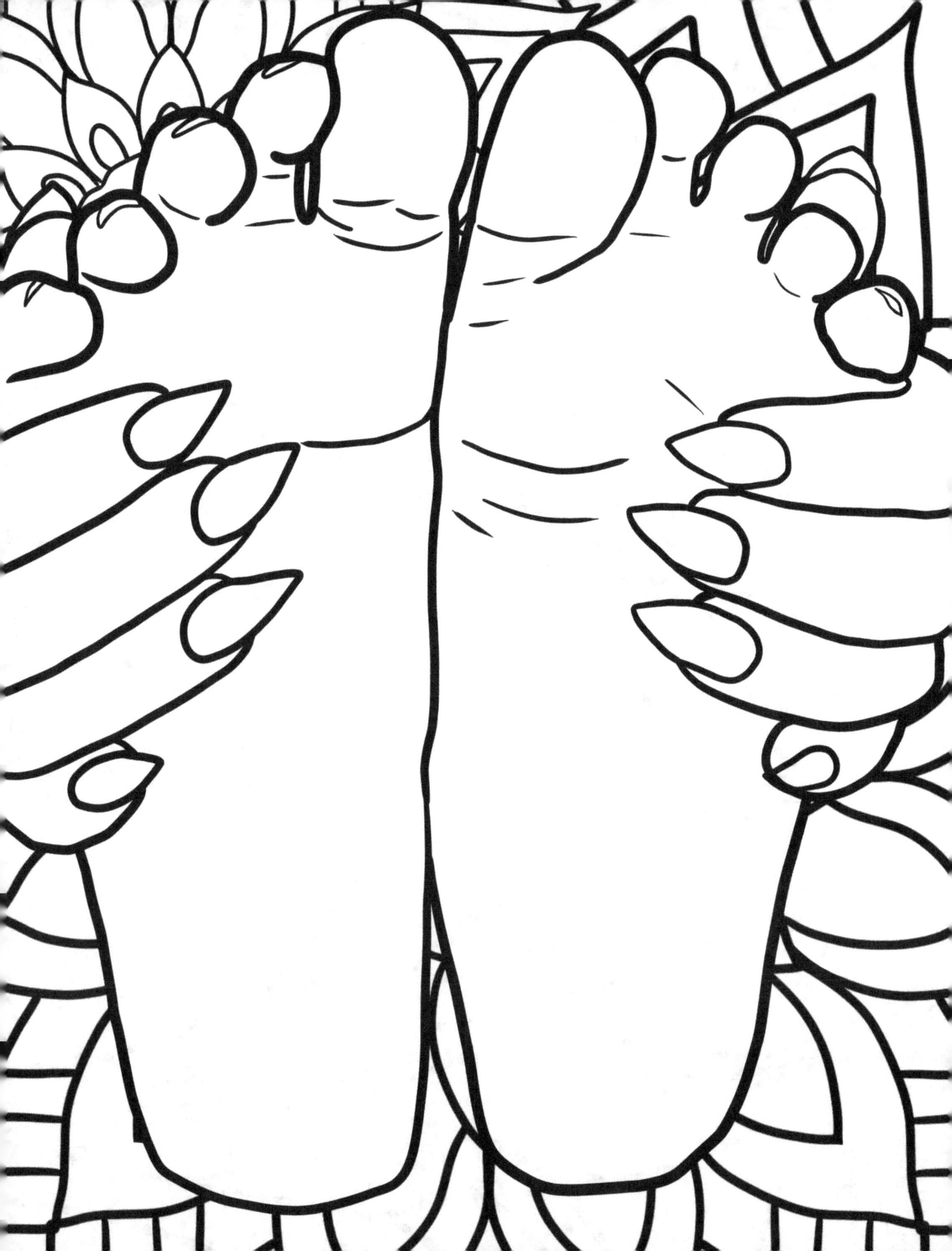

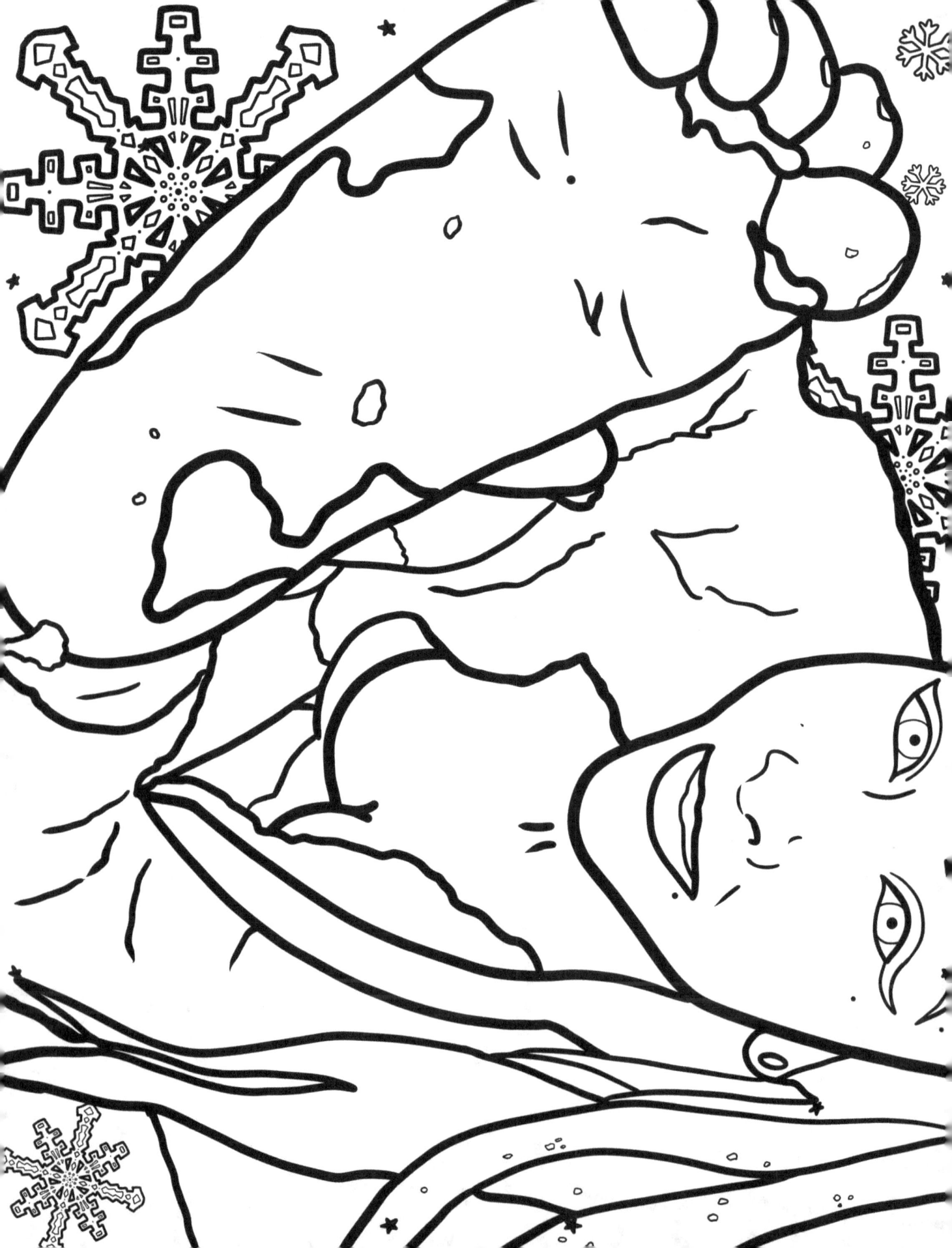

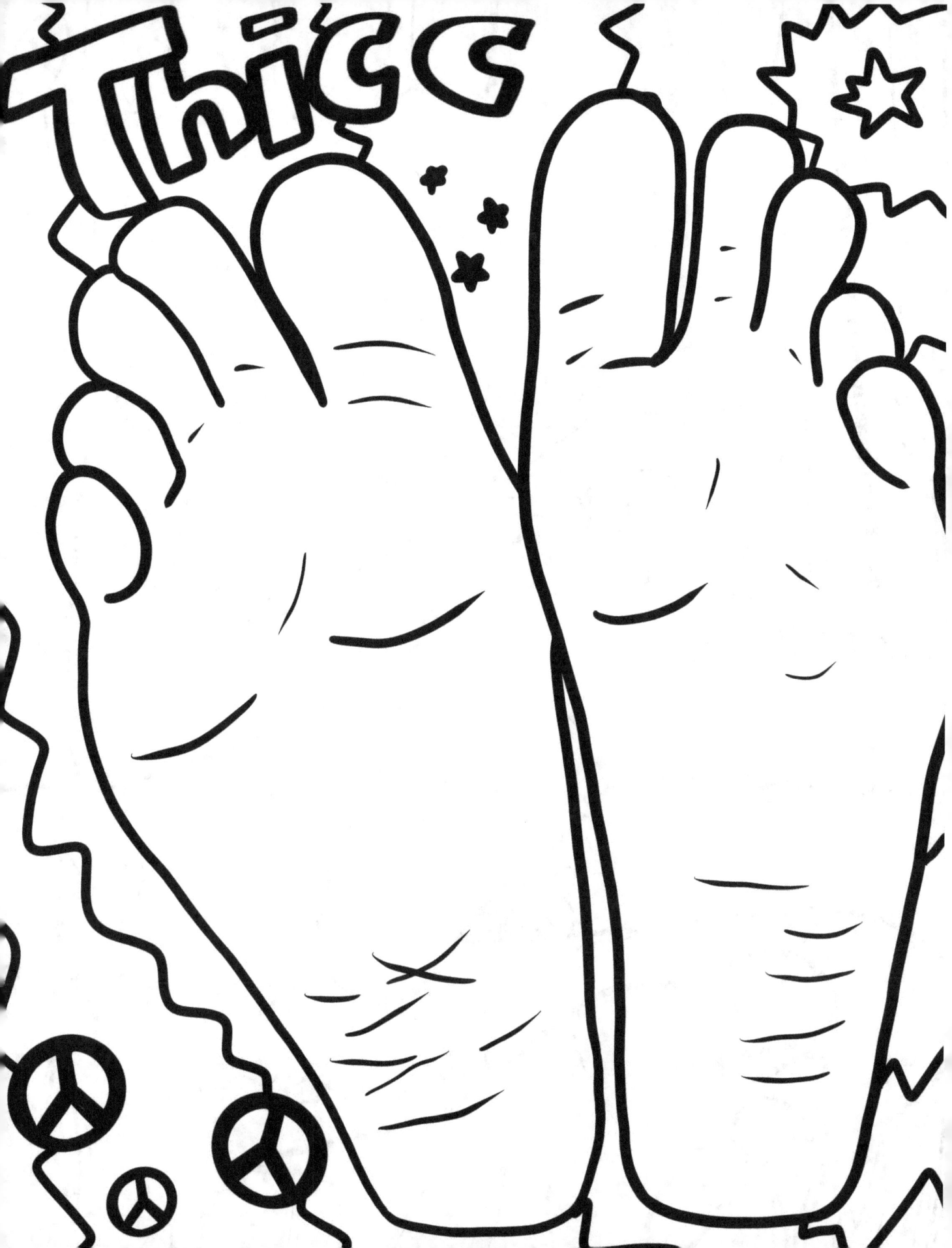

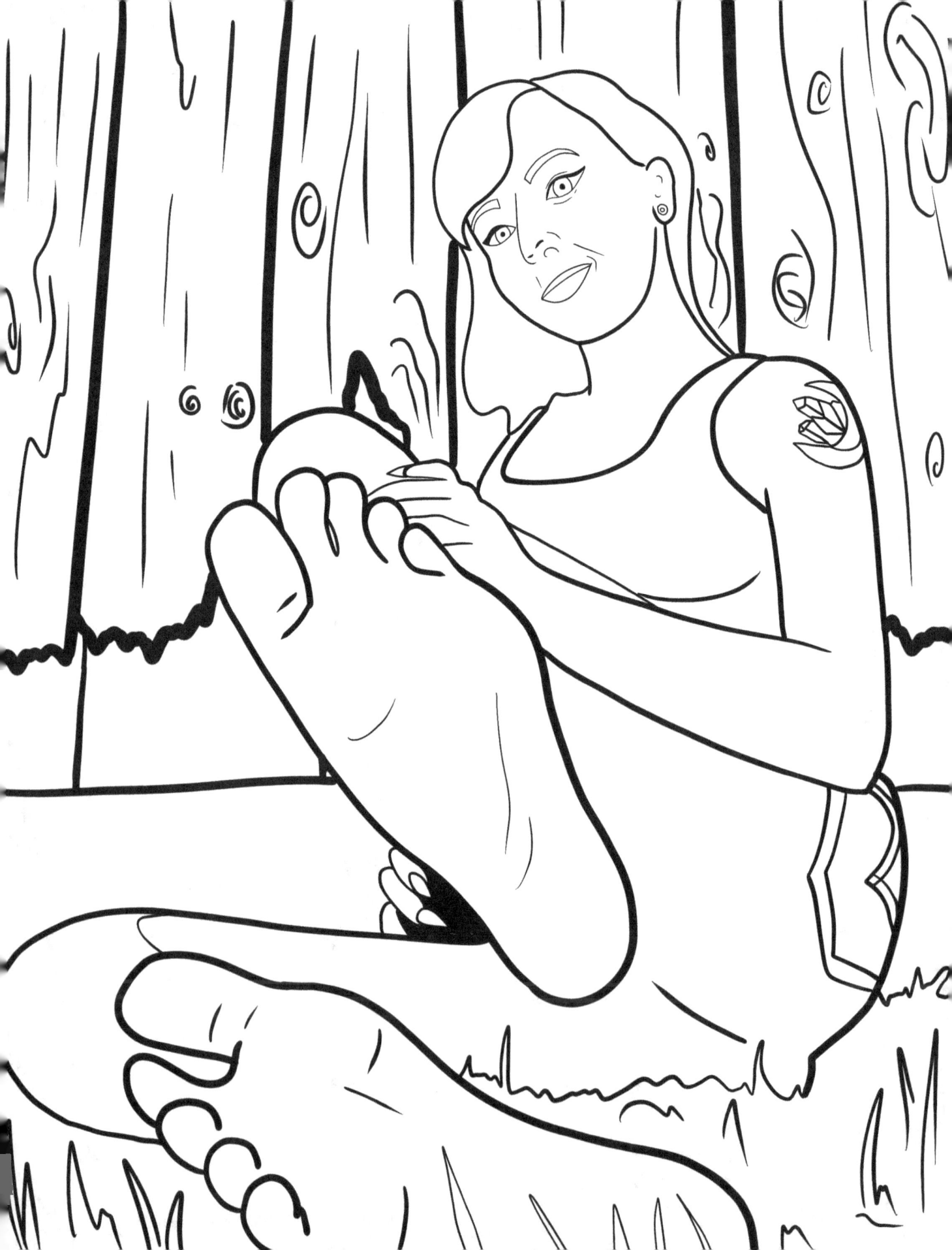

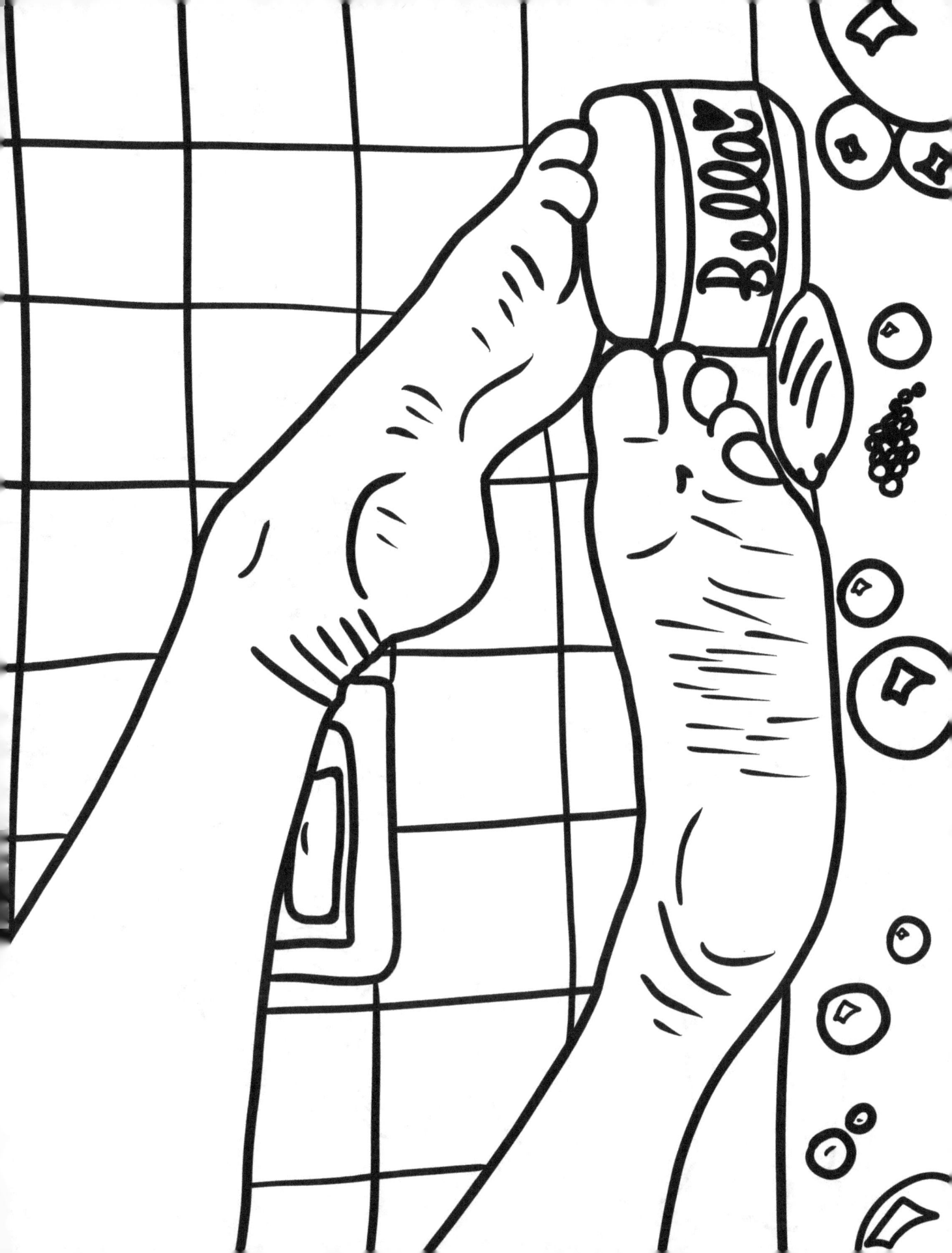

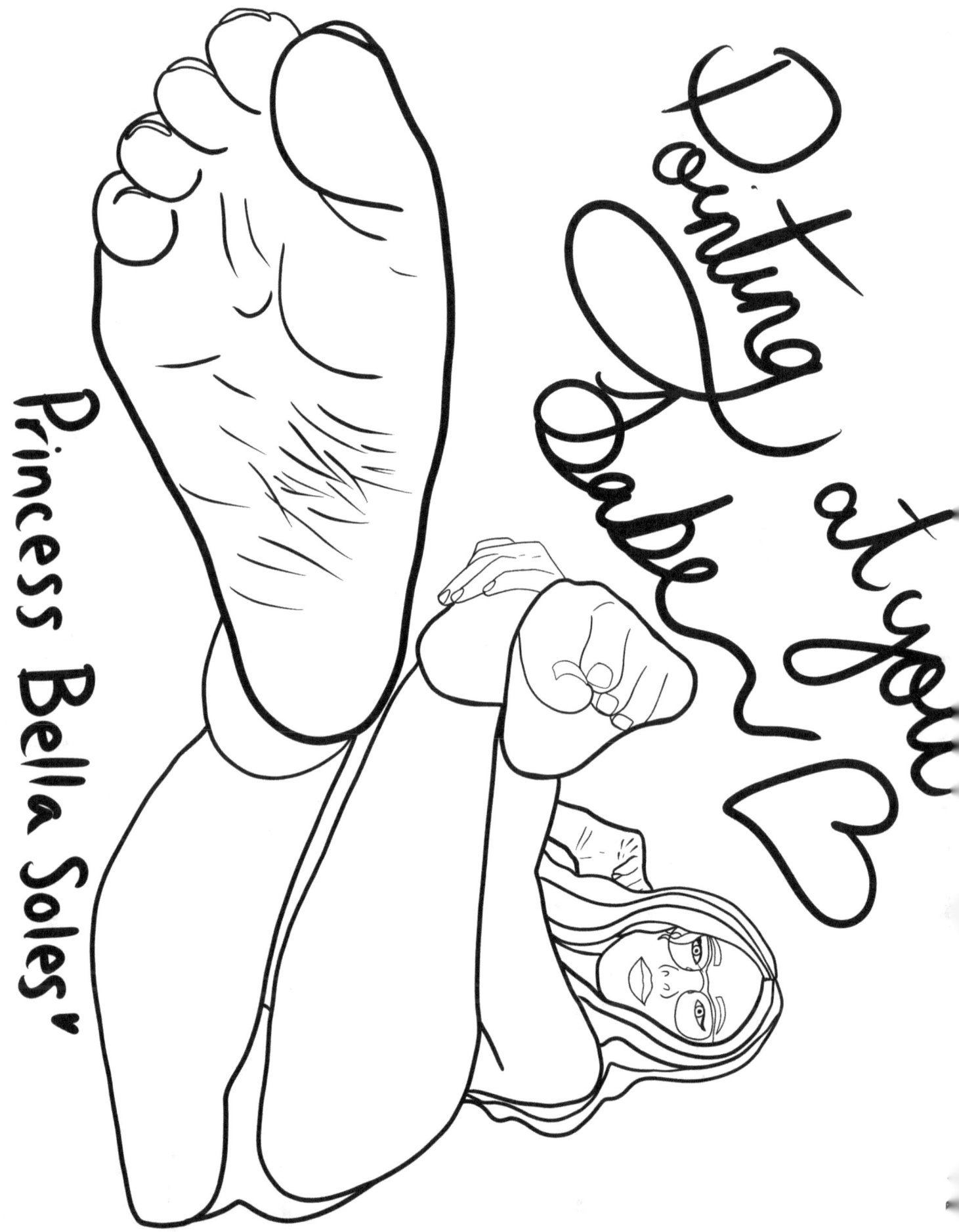

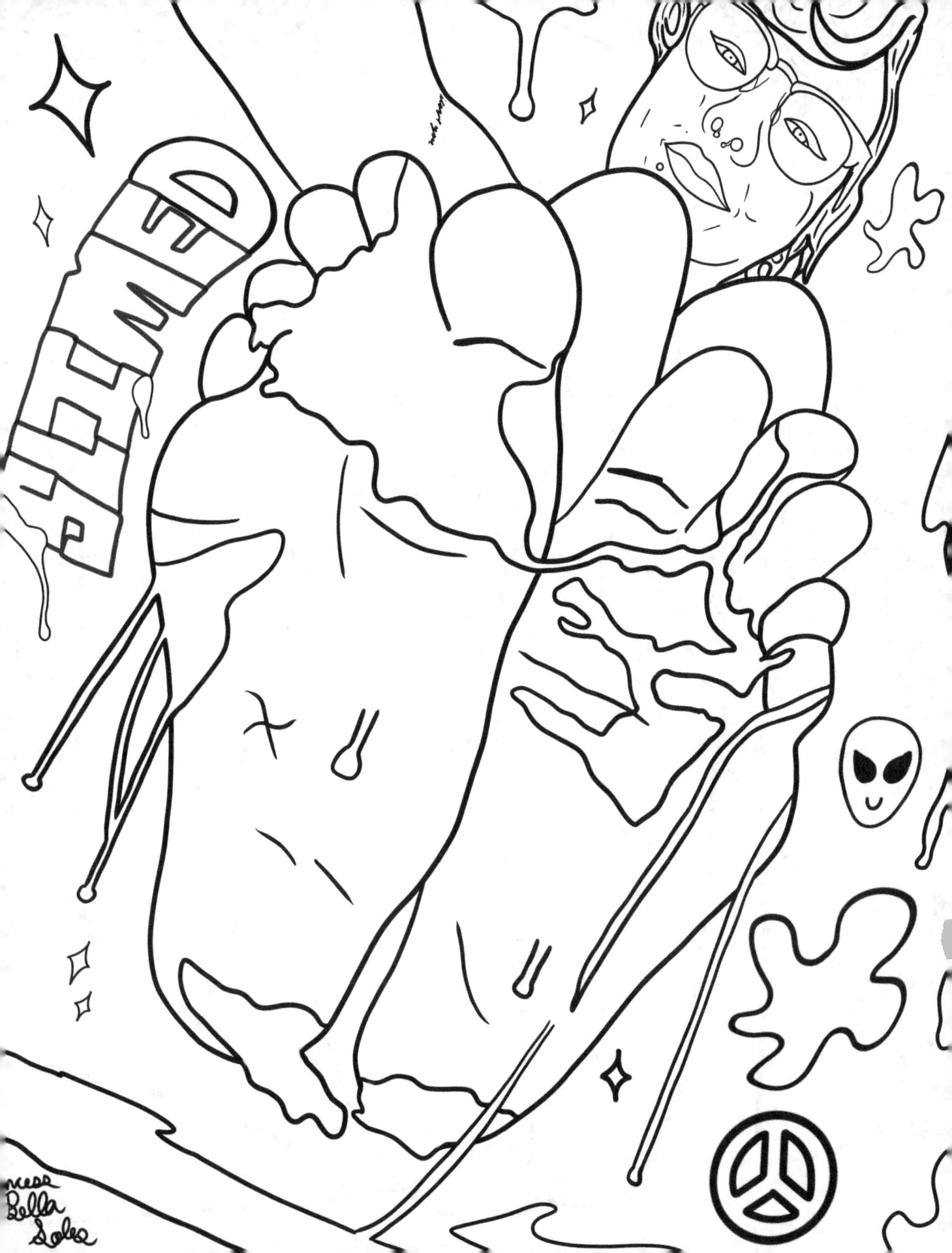

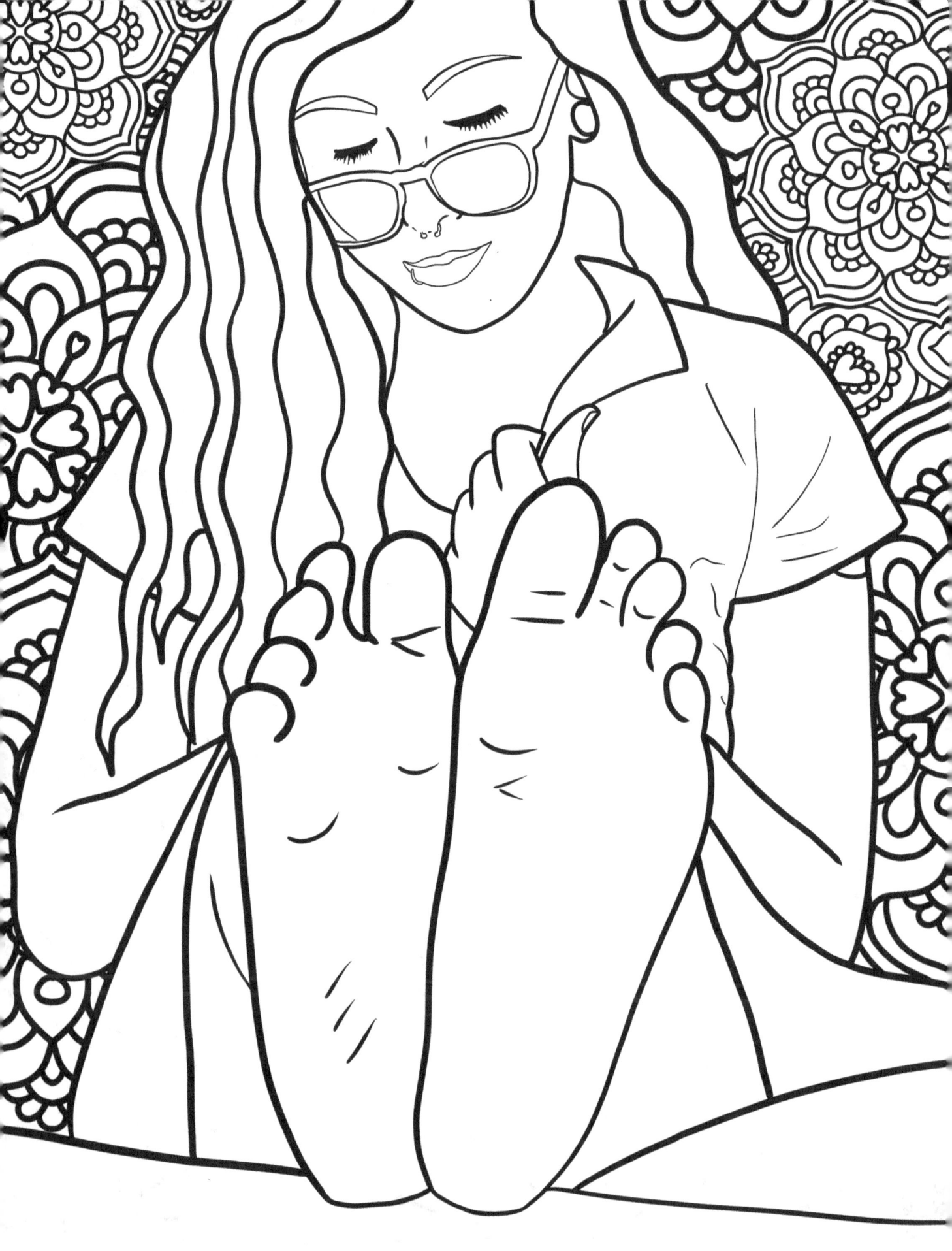

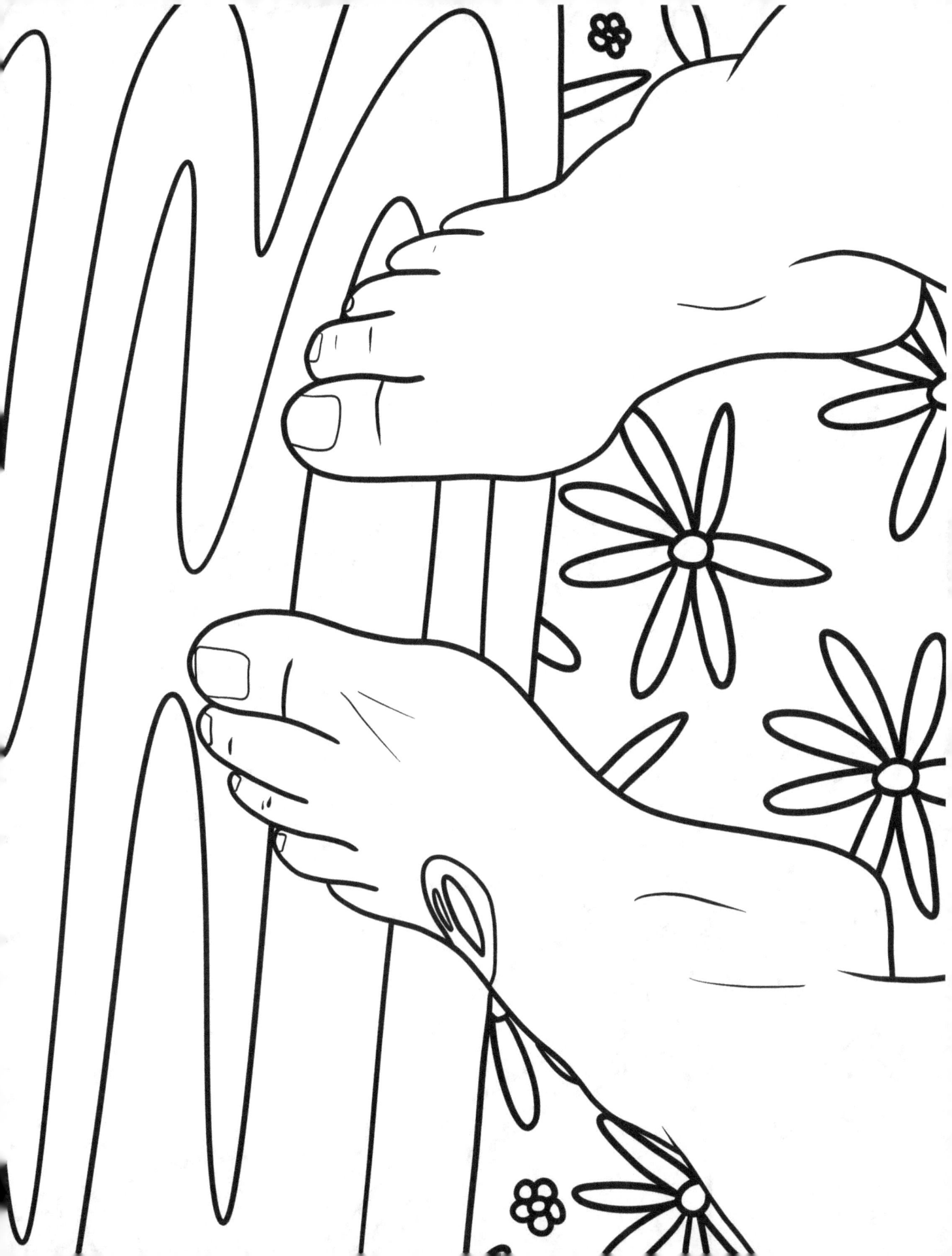

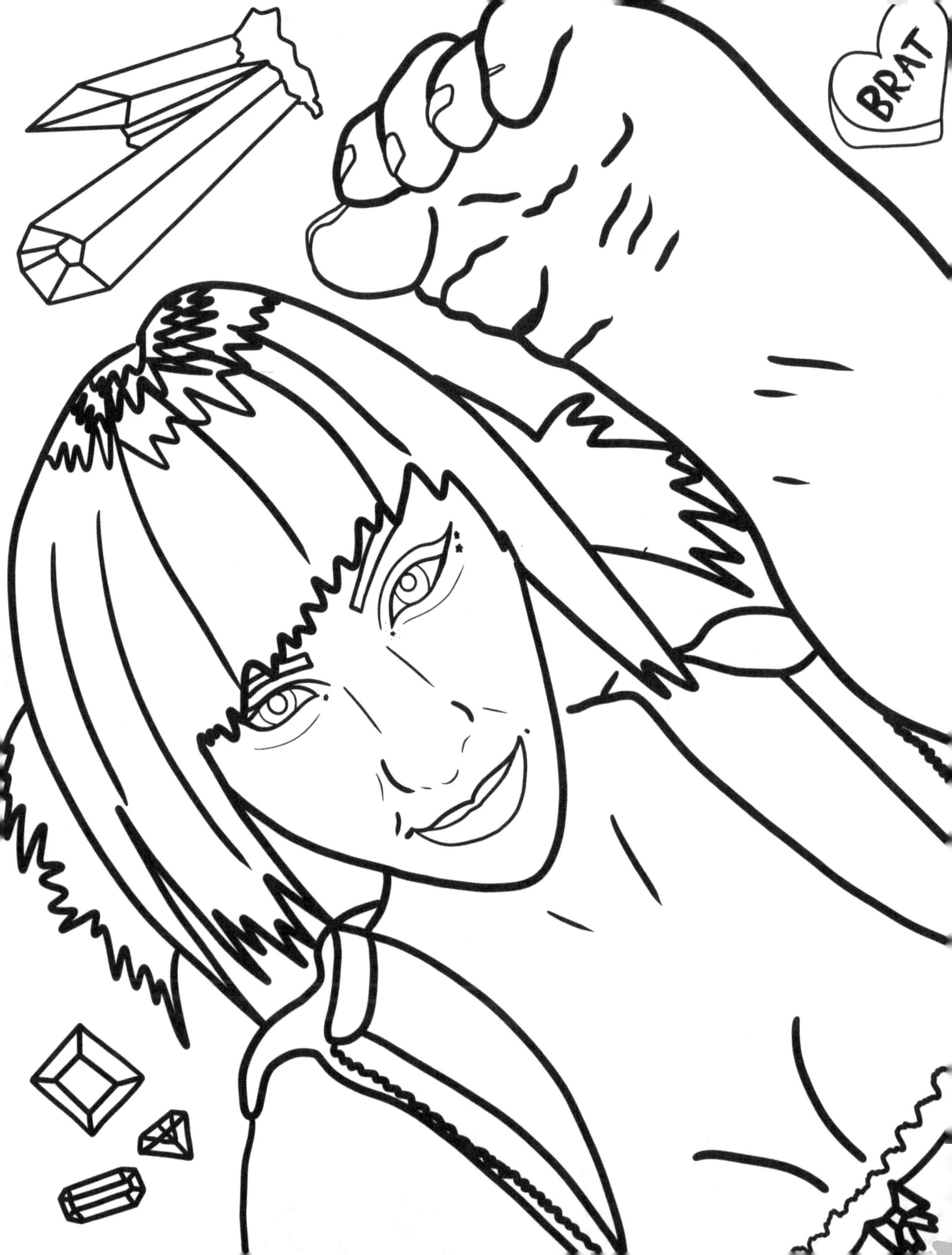

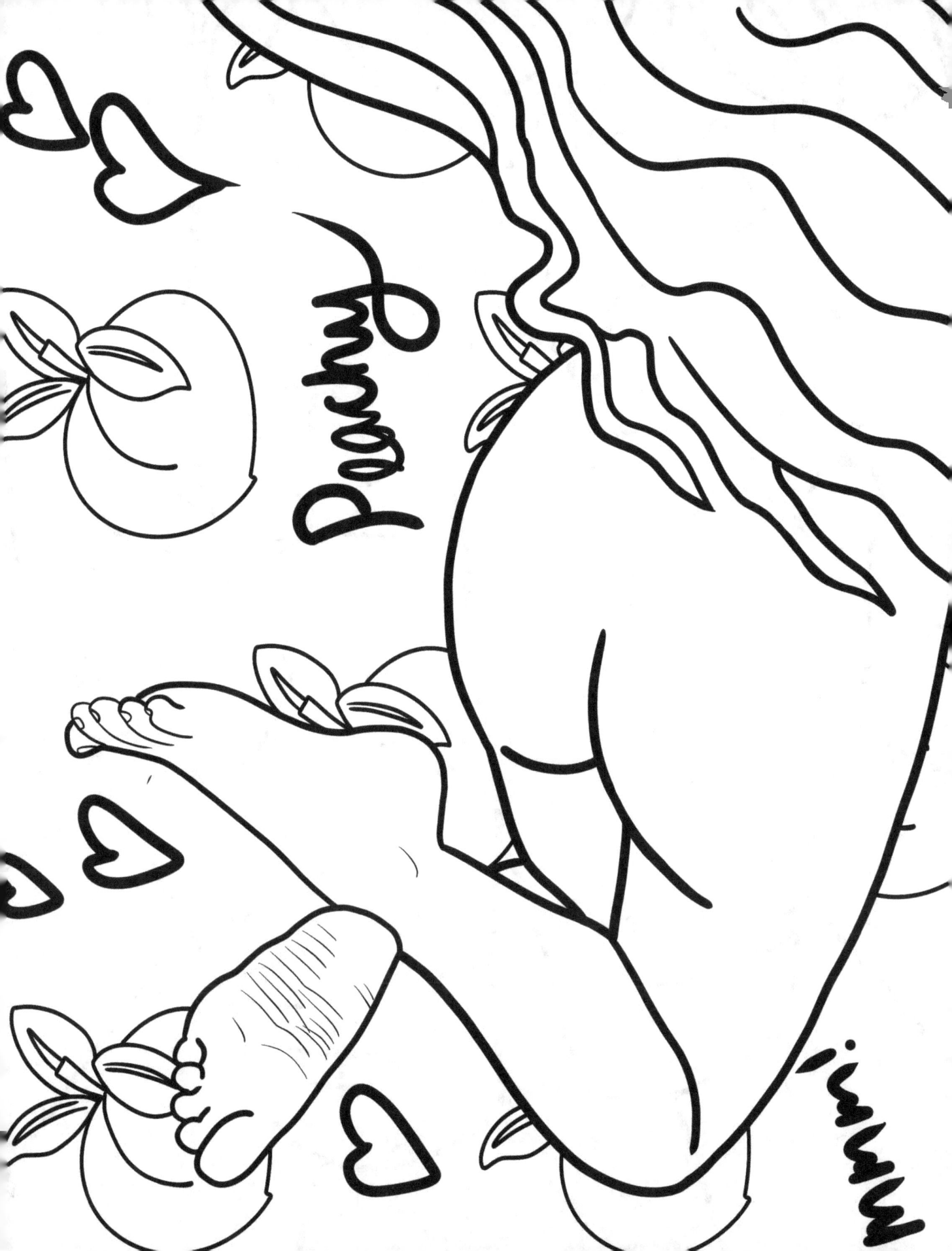

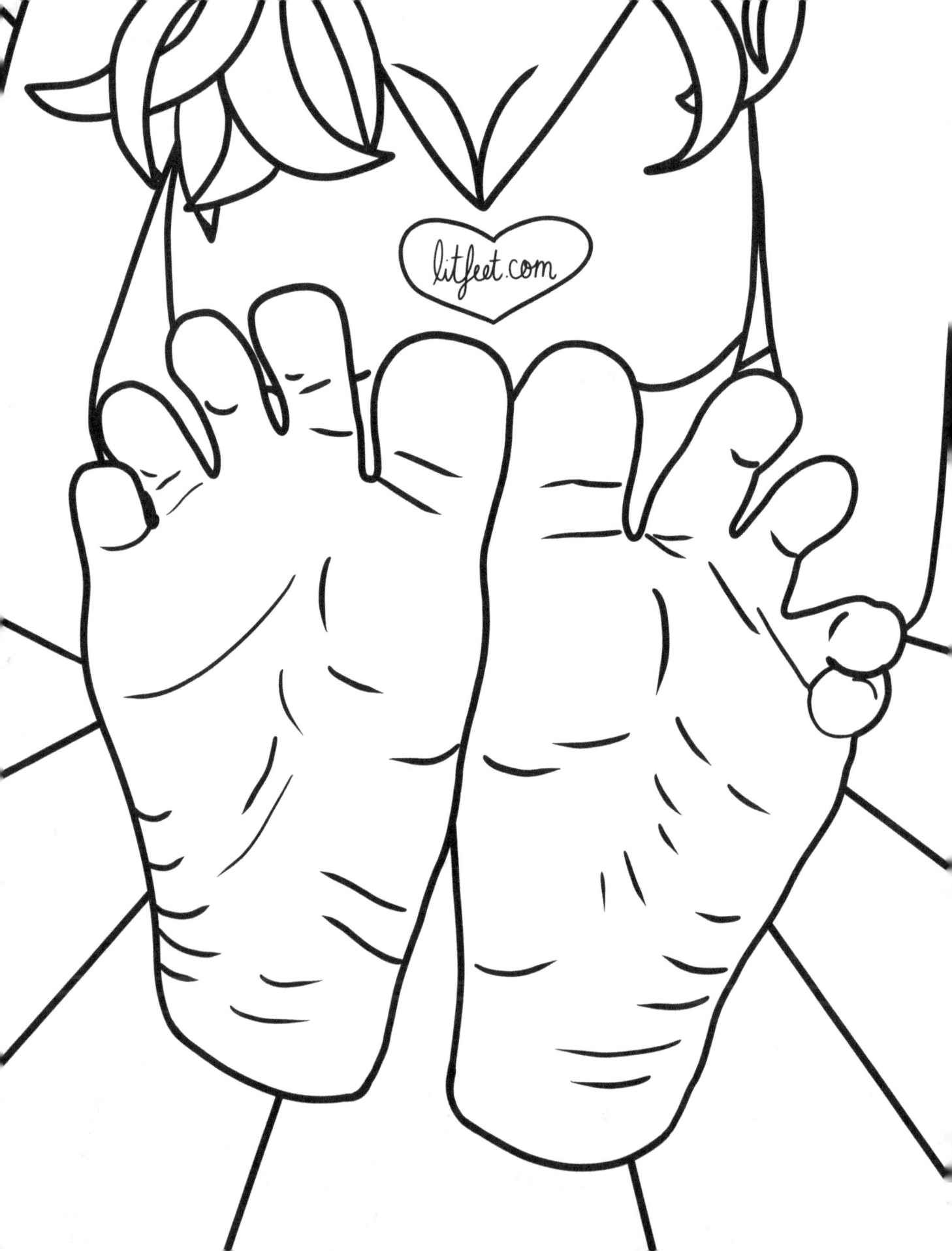

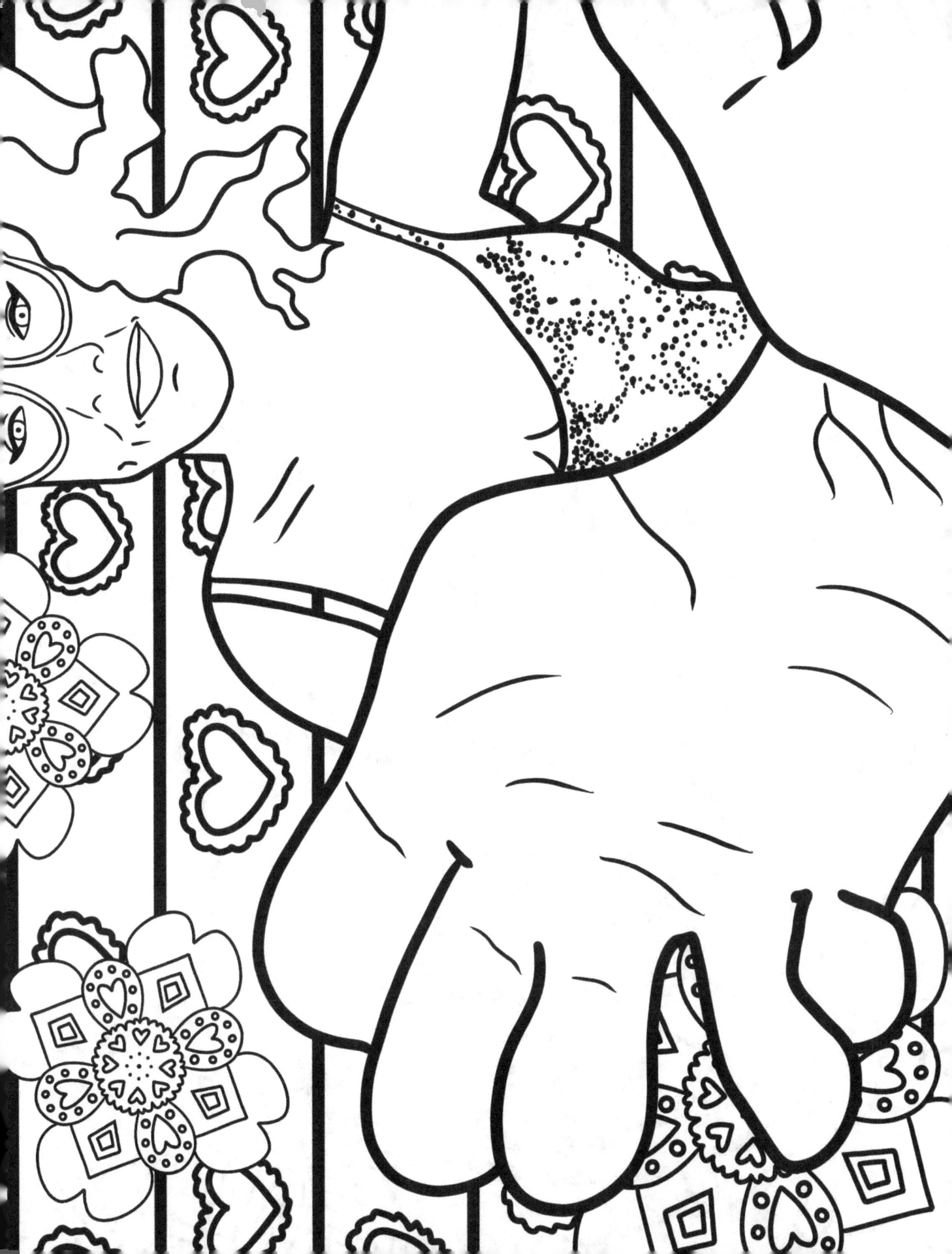

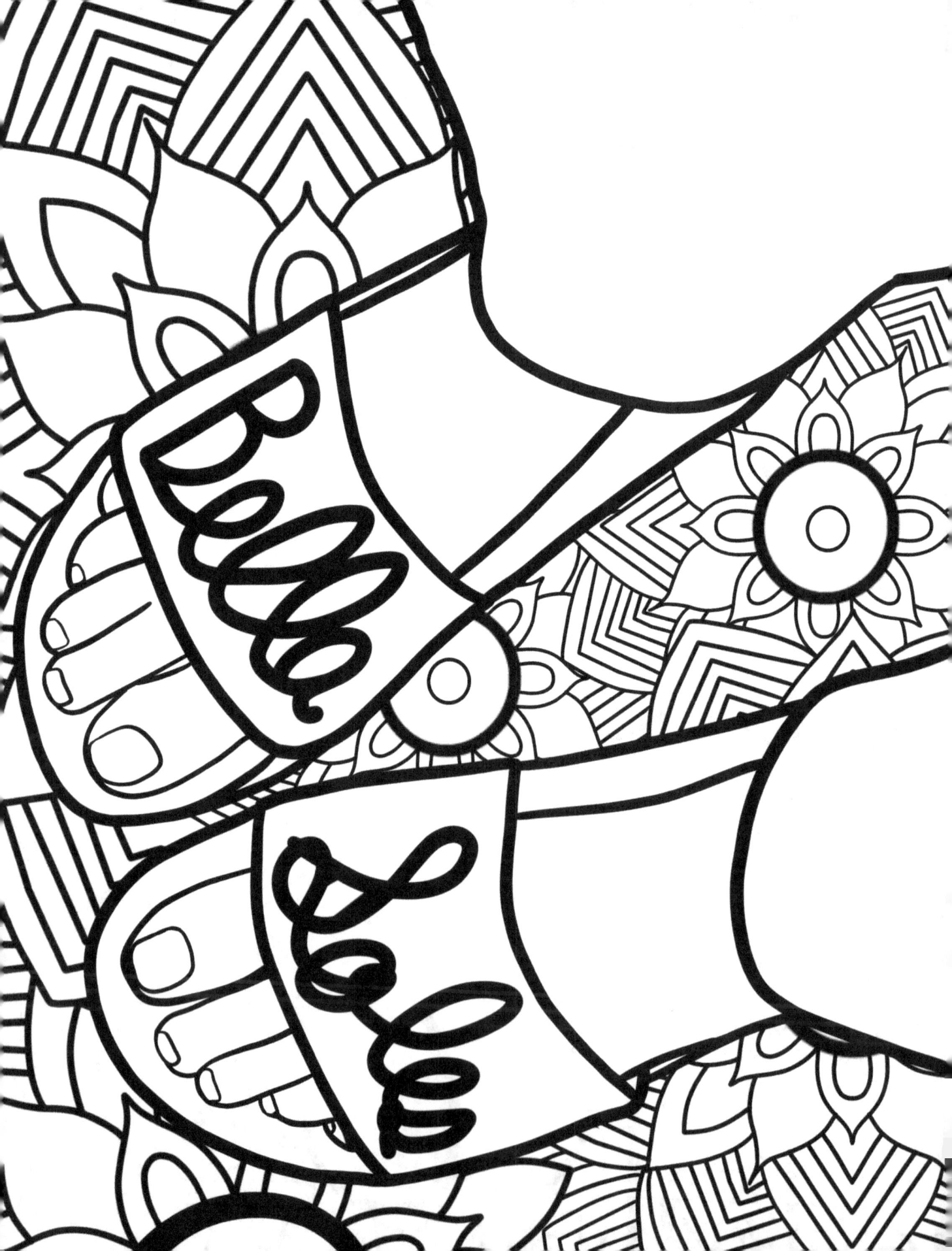

My Favorite Princess Bella Soles videos are...

1. Bratty Foot Babe Gets What She Deserves
2. Praising You For Loving Feet
3. _____
4. _____
5. _____
6. _____
7. _____
8. _____
9. _____
10. _____
11. _____
12. _____
13. _____
14. _____
15. _____

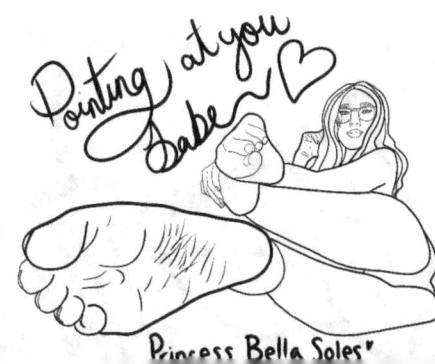

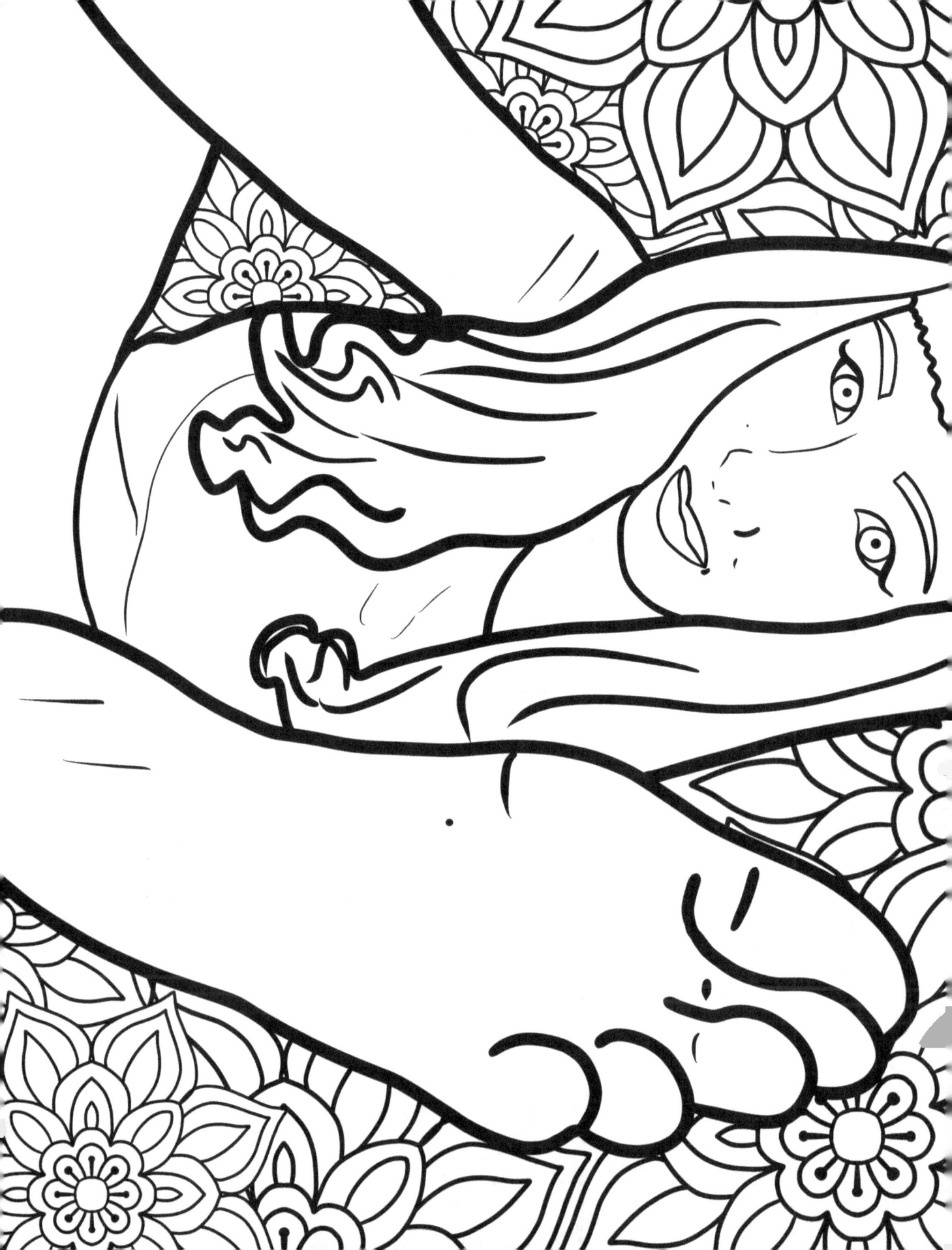

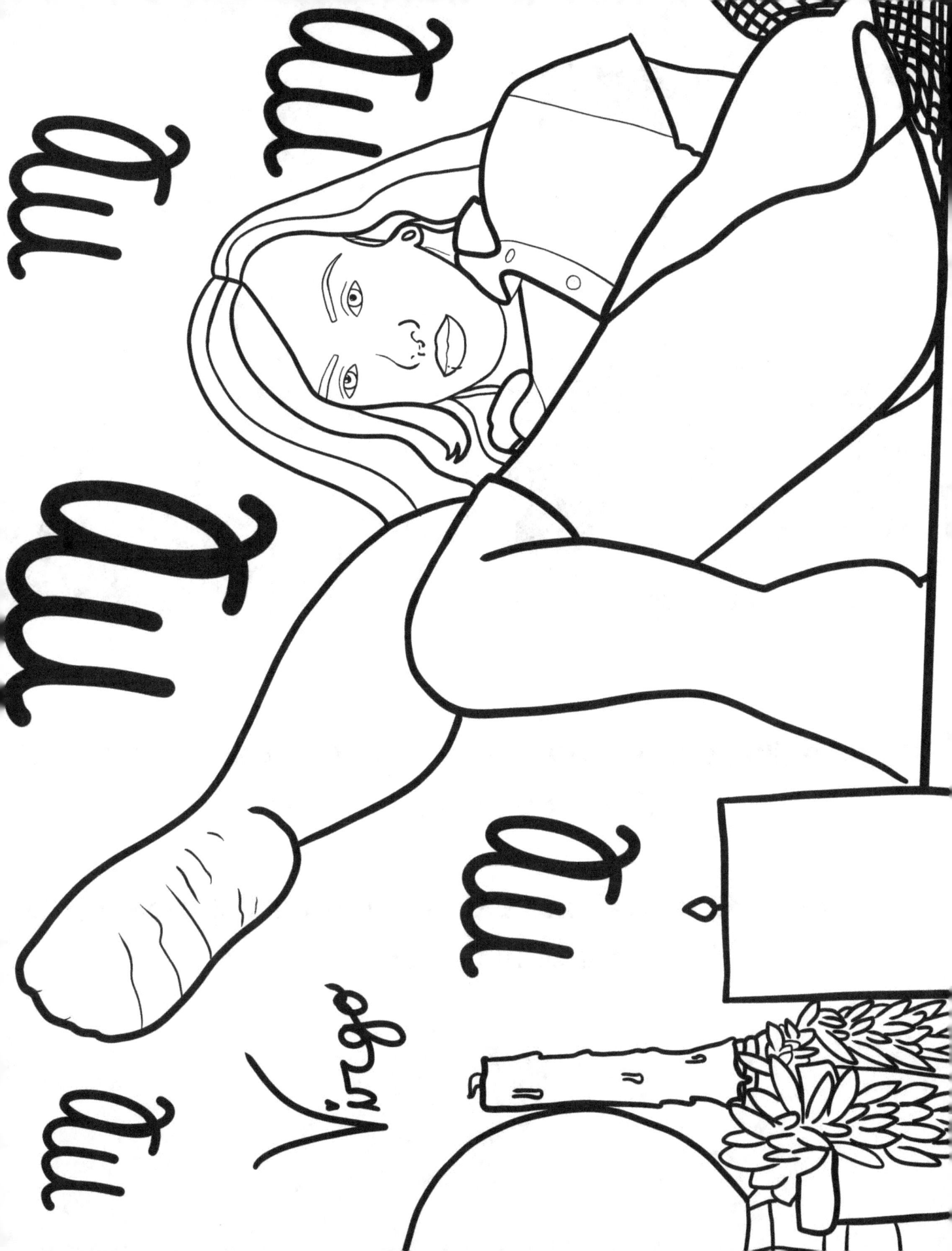

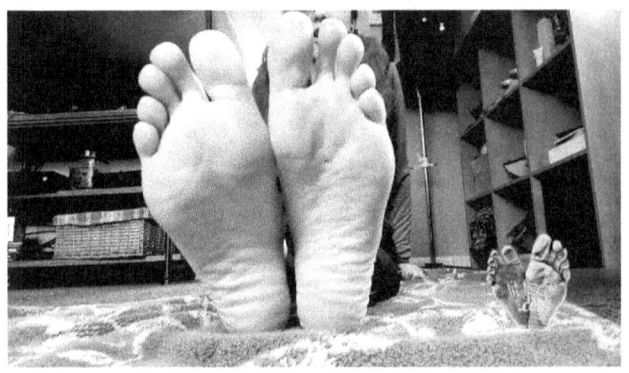

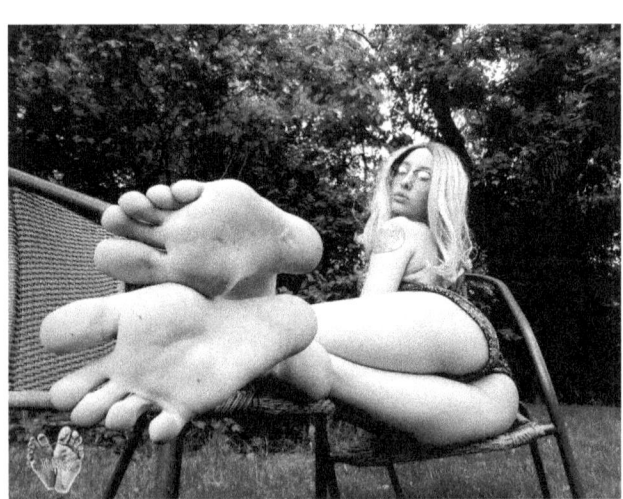

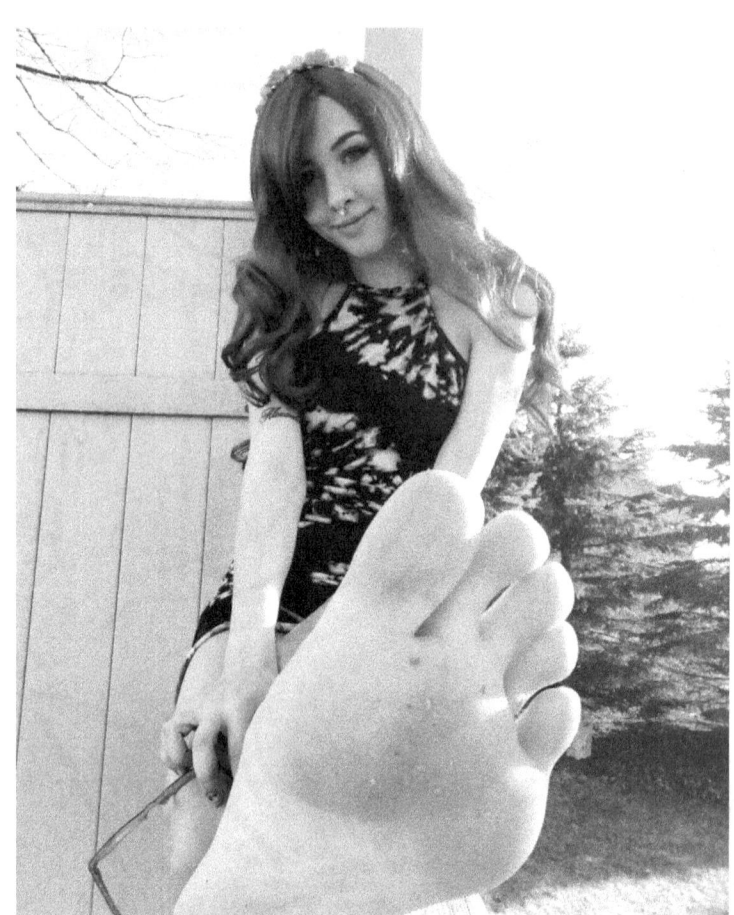

Please like, share, and follow Princess Bella Soles and Lit Feet on social media!

Visit the official website LitFeet.com for the most up to date info! Sign up for discounts!

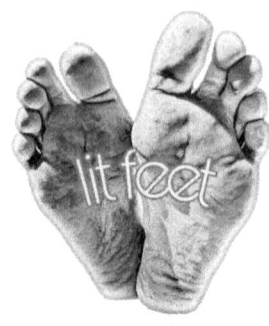

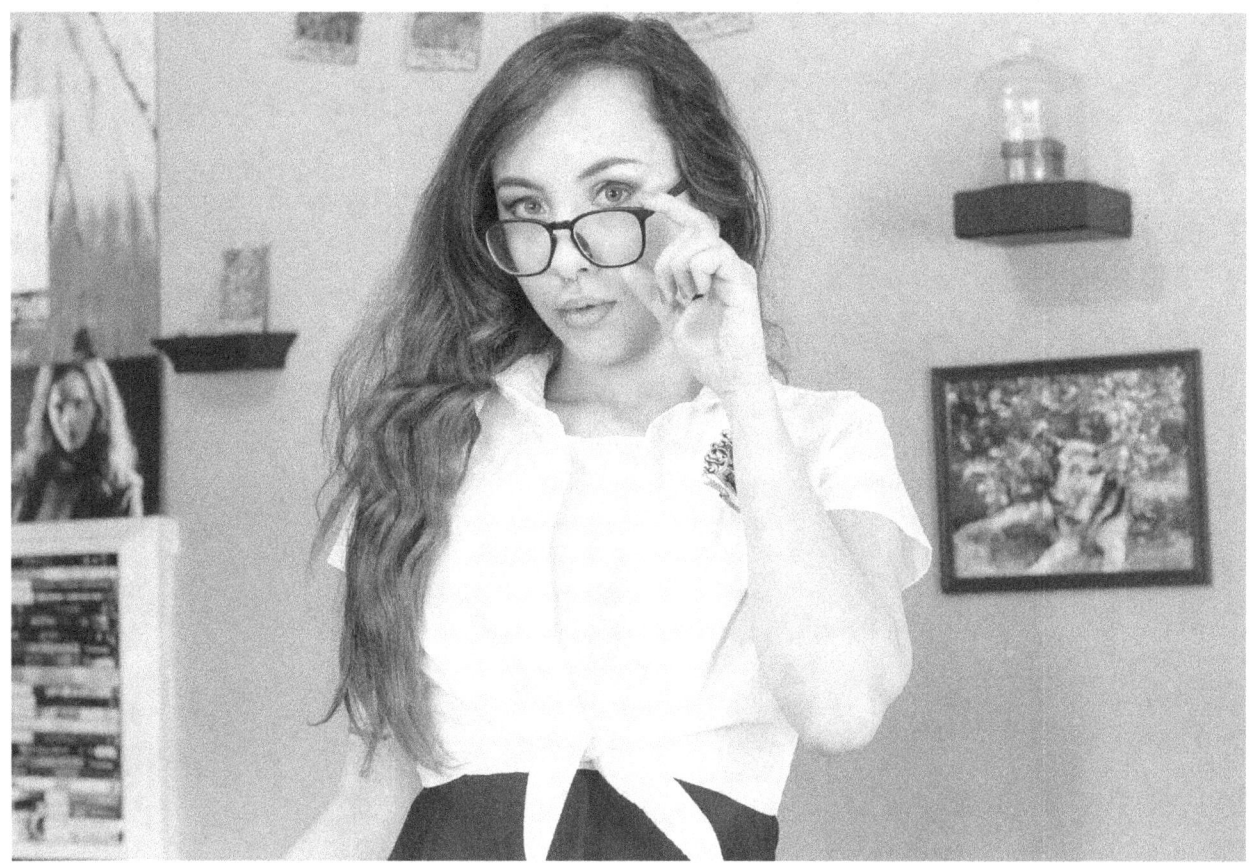

Princess Bella Soles is a woman of many facets. She is an artist first and foremost but also a model, photographer, producer, cosplayer, mentor, business owner, and much more. Based in the Midwest, Bella has gained many adoring fans throughout the world in the foot community. In this book, Bella has taken some her favorite self-portraits and hand drawn them for your pleasure. She hopes you find this book relaxing.

In her free time Bella enjoys going to rock concerts, foraging for mushrooms in the wilderness, and taking photos of wildlife.

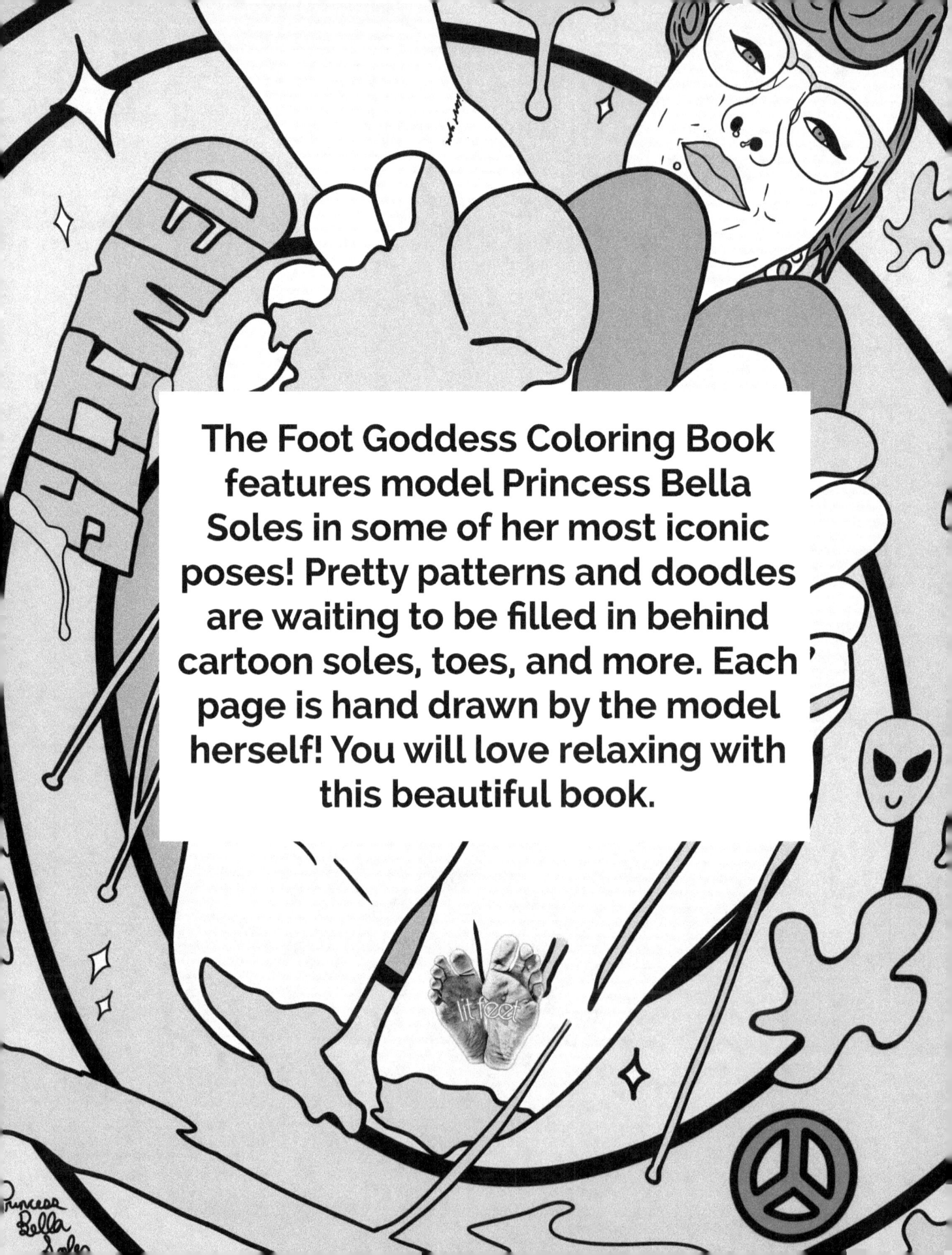